Mueller Austria Toaster Oven Cookbook

Quick, Easy, and Delicious Recipes for Your Mueller Austria Toaster Oven to Bake, Broil, and Toast

Brance Linous

Table of Contents

Introduction

You may have experienced a craving for perfectly melted cheese over crispy French fries but feels like it is too much work using a big oven for just a bowl.

Or perhaps you need to whip out a tasty meal right away to feed a horde of hungry and impatient children. Have no fear for the toaster is here.

Oven toasters are straightforward kitchen appliances that are excellent for when you want to toast, bake, broil, or heat food. You can easily melt cheese over a bowl of nachos, bake crispy-crusted pizza, and of course, toast your favorite breakfast bread to perfection. But you do not have to stop there.

Toaster ovens are well capable of handling a wide range of recipes you would not normally think possible. If you can fit it, you can most likely cook it in an oven toaster.

Many people usually associate oven toasters to breakfast foods, but these underrated cookers are much more versatile than that. You will easily find a toaster oven in households these days and for a good reason. They are compact and can quickly cook food without the hassle that comes with standard ovens that often require pre-heating.

Some people would prefer an oven toaster to a microwave oven since it is cheaper and can perform more functions. Foods re-heated in a microwave usually become soggy and less appealing to eat as opposed to a toaster that does a better job at browning and adding a delectable crisp.

Countertop ovens also use up less space and do not make your entire kitchen uncomfortably hot that usually happens when you use traditional ovens.

Chapter 1: An Overview

Toaster ovens are smaller versions of the traditional ovens we all grew up having in our homes.

Over the years, smaller and more portable versions of appliances have become available to suit the changing needs and times. Newer iterations are much more energy-efficient and developed with a higher regard for the environment.

What is the Mueller Oven Toaster?

Mueller's oven toaster is an easy-to-use tabletop cooker that can effortlessly fit in your kitchen. They have the proprietary 'even toast technology' and make use of convection cooking that helps in energy efficiency.

Despite its size, this toaster can fit four slices of bread or a small pizza thanks to its curved interiors. These toaster ovens from Mueller will also let you broil and bake your favorite meals quicker than a standard oven. It allows you to slow cook and keep your food warm.

The toaster can reach temperatures up to 450° F that is enough to bake small portions of meat and roast vegetables. This temperature range enables you to cook a variety of dishes from simple kale and garlic chips to savory dinners like glazed salmon and chicken kebabs.

How Does it Work?

Conventional ovens utilize the circulating dry air that emanates from heating elements usually found at the bottom and top.

Toaster ovens are tabletop versions of conventional ovens and sometimes equipped with convection fans for even distribution of heat and better cooking. The heating element at the bottom is used when the bake or toast option is selected while the top heating element is used for broiling purposes.

The biggest advantage of a toaster oven over its full-sized counterpart is the improved cooking time and energy consumption. Due to the toaster's size and convection fans, the cooking space can immediately heat up, thereby eliminating the longer pre-heat process that conventional ovens require.

This will also shorten the cooking time, letting you enjoy your meals promptly and with little effort. Toasters are convenient options for people who cook or heat food in smaller portions.

Oven toasters are easy to operate and clean with its detachable crumb tray. It is perfect for people who are beginners at cooking and those who value convenience. Toasters are energy efficient and will cut more than half the energy consumption of conventional ovens. It will also save you more money from your electric bills in the end.

They are also much less expensive than full-size ovens and are portable. Plus, since they are multi-purpose, you can cook most meals that you would normally cook in a conventional oven in a toaster.

Cooking Times for Different Food

A Mueller oven toaster's temperature range will let you cook foods from breakfast to dessert instantly and without any difficulty. Here are some dishes you can test out and enjoy on your new toaster.

- The classic toast takes only one and a half minute each side with the temperature set at 350° F.
- You can bake biscuits at 350° F for only 15 minutes.
- Make peanut butter cookies for only 8-10 minutes at a 350° F setting.
- Bake whole-wheat muffins with walnuts and your choice of fruit at 425° F for 20-25 minutes or until no muffin sticks to the toothpick.
- Frittatas require 350° F for a total of 35 minutes of cooking time in an oven toaster.
- Try out pizza bagels by setting your toaster to 375° F and cooking for only 8-10 minutes.
- Savory stuffed mushrooms with cheese are easy to make and requires a temperature of 375° F for 20 minutes on a bake setting.

- Roasted baby potatoes only needs 25 minutes of cook time at 400° F with occasional turning for an even roast.
- Placing eggs directly on the grates and choosing the bake setting with a temperature of 325° F for about 30 minutes will make hard-boiled eggs.
- You can make baked eggs in ramekins together with your choice of vegetables and condiments for 15 minutes with temperatures set at 375° F.
- Tuna or salmon sandwich only takes 3 minutes at 350° F or until the fish is cooked.
- You can make fish and chips by setting the toaster at 450° F for 8-12 minutes until the fish is thoroughly cooked.
- Pork kebabs require a temperature of 425° F for at least 25 minutes until the pork is well done.
- Sausages cook at 450° F for at least 10 minutes on each side but can be cooked longer depending on your preference. You will need to flip the sausages to get even browning.

What You Should Know Before Buying

The primary considerations in buying an oven toaster should be based on your intended use, food preference, and price. If you know that a standard-sized kitchen oven is too big for your everyday food selections, then a toaster oven will definitely be a better choice.

One of the first things to take into account is your ideal toaster's size. You have to regard the number of heads in your household and your kitchen counter space. Some toasters handle better capacity than smaller ones, although it is not apparent at first glance.

The size will spell the difference between utility and uselessness. If possible, opt for toasters that have a bigger capacity if you will be cooking for your family members or using it for a small business. Otherwise, a smaller toaster is suitable for one to two persons.

Your food preferences also play a part in choosing the type of toaster. Different models offer varying controls and settings that will determine which types of food you can cook. Although most standard toaster ovens are capable of handling everyday cooking tasks, you may still want to compare with other models to home in on the best option for your cooking needs.

Nowadays, tabletop cookers are fitted with advanced controls and capabilities that some people require but others may not need. To save you additional costs, you must also consider your purpose of getting one.

Most affordable toasters are capable of handling numerous functions and are equipped with standard controls that are in themselves sufficient. Some higher-end models may have added features, such as enhanced energy efficiency, bigger capacity, intuitive controls, LCD display, and additional settings that are food-specific.

Tips for Safety and Cooking Convenience

Just like any other kitchen appliance, toaster ovens must be operated according to the manufacturer's guidelines to ensure safety. Once you got your brand-new unit, make sure that you review the manual before cooking with your oven toaster. Here are some useful tips to guide you.

- Only buy from reputable brands to take advantage of warranties and servicing. Look for the NSF certification as this ensures that the toaster has passed stringent product testing for health standards, safety, materials, and durability.
- Before attempting to clean your toaster, unplug it and let it completely cool. Never leave your appliance plugged in when not in use.
- Place your toaster in a stable and level countertop that can withstand heat. It should be somewhere away from the traffic in your kitchen.
- Position the toaster oven where small children cannot reach and away from areas that usually get wet. Leave some ample space around the oven toaster to let air easily cool it. Avoid placing any flammable or plastic materials that may easily melt or catch fire with high temperatures.
- Do not use tongs, ladles, and utensils made of metal. Choose oven-safe materials to avoid the risk of electric shock.
- Clean your toaster after each use, or whenever necessary, to maintain its lifespan

and keep it working at optimum performance. Some foods are just messier to cook and may cause drippings to reach the heating elements below. You just have to clean this immediately to avoid build-up that may cause heat fluctuations and worse a fire.

- You can use regular items found around the house to clean the toaster, such as baking soda, vinegar, lemon, and dish soap. Use an old toothbrush and a mixture of baking soda and water to clean the heating elements when they get too grimy. Do not use scouring pads or brushes made of metal as they pose a risk of electrocution.

- Take out all the trays first, then wash and air-dry them before putting them back. Do not get the inside of the oven soaked.

Let's get started cooking!

Chapter 2: 21-Day Meal plan

Day 1

Breakfast: Blueberry muffins

Lunch: Herbed beef tenderloin

Dinner: Broiled salmon with zucchini

Day 2

Breakfast: Breakfast hash

Lunch: Brussels sprouts with creamy cheese sauce

Dinner: Broiled steak

Day 3

Breakfast: French toast

Lunch: Cheesesteak sandwich

Dinner: Grilled pork belly

Day 4

Breakfast: Breakfast tart

Lunch: Char Siu pork

Dinner: Miso-glazed salmon

Day 5

Breakfast: Greek frittata

Lunch: Meatloaf

Dinner: Baked pork chops

Day 6

Breakfast: Baked marinara eggs

Lunch: Glazed pork tenderloin

Dinner: Garlic chicken

Day 7

Breakfast: Breakfast sandwich

Lunch: Baked crispy chicken

Dinner: Cajun pork chops

Day 8

Breakfast: Baked eggs and mushrooms

Lunch: Broiled steak

Dinner: Baked cheesy salmon

Day 9

Breakfast: Egg and bacon toast cups

Lunch: Shredded chicken

Dinner: Turkey meatloaf

Day 10

Breakfast: Breakfast tart

Lunch: Grilled pork belly

Dinner: Cordon bleu

Day 11

Breakfast: Sunny side up eggs

Lunch: Veggie stuffed red bell peppers

Dinner: Baked chicken taters

Day 12

Breakfast: Blueberry muffins

Lunch: Parmesan chicken

Dinner: Broiled salmon with zucchini

Day 13

Breakfast: Greek frittata

Lunch: Herbed beef tenderloin

Dinner: Pesto salmon

Day 14

Breakfast: Baked marinara eggs

Lunch: Chicken and veggies with rosemary

Dinner: Parmesan fish fillet

Day 15

Breakfast: Baked eggs and mushrooms

Lunch: Chicken casserole

Dinner: Baked sole and asparagus

Day 16

Breakfast: Sunny side up eggs

Lunch: Mustard salmon with green beans

Dinner: Char Siu pork

Day 17

Breakfast: French toast

Lunch: Scalloped potatoes

Dinner: Garlic herb pork

Day 18

Breakfast: Egg and bacon toast cups

Lunch: Brussels sprouts with creamy cheese sauce

Dinner: Lemon butter shrimp

Day 19

Breakfast: Blueberry muffins

Lunch: Broiled tilapia with avocado

Dinner: Baked crispy chicken

Day 20

Breakfast: Breakfast sandwich

Lunch: Cajun pork chops

Dinner: Baked chicken strips

Day 21

Breakfast: Breakfast hash

Lunch: Broiled steak

Dinner: Walnut-crusted salmon

Chapter 3: Breakfast

Breakfast Tart

Preparation Time: 15 minutes

Cooking Time: 30 minutes

Servings: 4

Ingredients:

- 1 9 x 13-inch puff pastry sheet
- 1/2 cup cheddar cheese, shredded
- 7 strips bacon, cooked crispy and chopped
- 1/2 cup spinach, cooked
- 4 eggs

Method:

1. Preheat your toaster oven to 400 degrees F.
2. Add the puff pastry sheet to a small pan.
3. Pierce the center with a fork.
4. Bake it for 10 minutes.
5. Take it out of the oven.
6. Sprinkle cheddar cheese on top.
7. Top with the bacon and spinach.
8. Crack eggs in the middle.
9. Bake for 15 minutes.
10. Let cool before serving.

Serving Suggestion: Garnish with chopped onion chives before serving.

Preparation / Cooking Tips: Steam the spinach instead of boiling to preserve its nutrients.

Breakfast Sandwich

Preparation Time: 5 minutes
Cooking Time: 10 minutes
Serving: 1

Ingredients:

- Oil for greasing
- 1 egg
- Salt and pepper to taste
- 1 English muffin, sliced in two
- 1 slice Provolone cheese

Method:

1. Grease a small baking pan with oil.
2. Crack the egg into the pan.
3. Sprinkle with salt and pepper.
4. Bake the egg in the toaster oven until yolk is firm.
5. Toast the muffin until golden.
6. Put the egg on top of the muffin and add the cheese.

Serving Suggestion: Serve with fresh green salad.

Preparation / Cooking Tips: You can also season egg with dried herbs like basil.

Egg & Bacon Toast Cups

Preparation Time: 10 minutes

Cooking Time: 20 minutes

Servings: 4

Ingredients:

- Cooking spray
- 2 slices whole-wheat bread, crust trimmed and slice into 2
- 4 strips bacon, cooked crispy
- 4 eggs
- Salt and pepper to taste

Method:

1. Spray your muffin pan with oil.
2. Press bread into the muffin cups.
3. Add the bacon on top of the bread.
4. Crack the egg into each muffin cup.
5. Sprinkle with salt and pepper.
6. Cook in the toaster oven at 350 degrees F for 15 to 20 minutes.

Serving Suggestion: Sprinkle with chopped fresh herbs before serving.

Preparation / Cooking Tips: Use turkey bacon to enjoy a dish that's lower in fat and fewer in calories.

Blueberry Muffins

Preparation Time: 15 minutes
Cooking Time: 30 minutes
Servings: 4

Ingredients:

- Cooking spray
- 1/2 cup buttermilk
- 1 egg
- 2 tablespoons sugar
- 2 tablespoons applesauce
- 1/3 cup cornmeal
- 2/3 cup whole wheat flour
- 2 teaspoons baking powder
- Pinch salt
- Pinch cinnamon powder
- 1/2 cup blueberries

Method:

1. Spray muffin pan with oil.
2. Preheat your toaster oven to 350 degrees F.
3. In a bowl, combine all the ingredients.
4. Pour mixture into the muffin cups.
5. Bake for 25 to 30 minutes or until fully cooked.

Serving Suggestion: Serve with fresh fruits.

Preparation / Cooking Tips: You can also use other berries like raspberries or blackberries for this recipe.

French Toast

Preparation Time: 15 minutes

Cooking Time: 15 minutes

Servings: 4

Ingredients:

- 2 slices bread
- 2 teaspoons sugar
- ½ cup milk
- 2 eggs, beaten

Method:

1. Preheat your toaster oven to 350 degrees F.
2. In a bowl, mix the sugar, milk and eggs.
3. Dip the bread slices into the mixture.
4. Bake in the oven for 6 to 7 minutes per side.

Serving Suggestion: Sprinkle with cinnamon powder before serving.

Preparation / Cooking Tips: Use day-old bread for better results.

Baked Marinara Eggs

Preparation Time: 15 minutes

Cooking Time: 15 minutes

Servings: 6

Ingredients:

- Butter for greasing
- 6 eggs
- 1 cup marinara sauce
- 1/4 cup all-purpose cream
- 1/4 cup Parmesan cheese, shredded
- Salt and pepper to taste

Method:

1. Grease muffin pan with butter.
2. Preheat your toaster oven to 400 degrees F.
3. Pour marinara into the muffin cups.
4. Crack an egg into each of the muffin cup.
5. Top with cream and cheese.
6. Season with salt and pepper.
7. Bake in the oven for 15 minutes.

Serving Suggestion: Garnish with chopped chives. Serve with toasted garlic bread.

Preparation / Cooking Tips: Bake for a few more minutes until yolks are firm.

Greek Frittata

Preparation Time: 15 minutes

Cooking Time: 30 minutes

Servings: 4

Ingredients:

- 1 tablespoon olive oil
- 10 eggs
- Salt and pepper to taste
- 4 scallions, chopped
- 1-pint cherry tomatoes, sliced in half
- 5 oz. baby spinach, cooked
- 8 oz. feta, crumbled

Method:

1. Preheat your toaster oven to 350 degrees F.
2. Grease casserole dish with olive oil.
3. In a bowl, beat the eggs and season with salt and pepper.
4. Stir in the rest of the ingredients.
5. Pour mixture into the dish.
6. Bake for 30 minutes.

Serving Suggestion: Serve with toasted bread.

Preparation / Cooking Tips: You can also use other types of soft cheese for this recipe.

Breakfast Hash

Preparation Time: 5 minutes

Cooking Time: 25 minutes

Serving: 1

Ingredients:

- 2 slices bacon, cooked
- 4 potatoes, sliced and boiled
- 1 egg
- 1/4 cup cheddar cheese, shredded

Method:

1. Add bacon strips to a small baking pan.
2. Top with the potatoes.
3. Crack an egg on top.
4. Bake in the toaster oven at 350 degrees F for 20 minutes.
5. Sprinkle cheese on top and bake for another 5 minutes.

Serving Suggestion: Serve with toasted bread.

Preparation / Cooking Tips: You can also beat the egg before pouring on top of the potatoes.

Sunny Side Up Eggs

Preparation Time: 5 minutes

Cooking Time: 15 minutes

Serving: 1

Ingredients:

- Cooking spray
- 2 eggs
- Salt and pepper to taste

Method:

1. Spray a small baking pan with oil.
2. Crack 2 eggs into the prepared pan.
3. Bake the eggs for 15 minutes.
4. Season with salt and pepper.

Serving Suggestion: Sprinkle with dried herbs on top before serving.

Preparation / Cooking Tips: You can cook more than one egg at a time.

Baked Eggs & Mushrooms

Preparation Time: 10 minutes

Cooking Time: 15 minutes

Servings: 4

Ingredients:

- 1 tablespoon butter
- 1 onion, chopped
- 1/2 cup mushrooms
- 2 slices ham, chopped
- 1 cup baby spinach
- 4 eggs
- Salt and pepper to taste
- 1 cup mozzarella cheese, grated

Method:

1. Add butter to a pan over medium heat.
2. Cook onion, mushrooms and ham for 3 to 5 minutes, stirring.
3. Stir in spinach.
4. Cook for 2 minutes.
5. Pour mixture into a muffin pan.
6. Crack eggs into each muffin cup.
7. Season with salt and pepper.
8. Bake in the toaster oven at 375 degrees F for 15 minutes.
9. Sprinkle with cheese and bake for another 5 minutes.

Serving Suggestion: Serve with bread or salad.

Preparation / Cooking Tips: You can also use other types of cheese for this recipe.

Chapter 4: Meat

Broiled Steak

Preparation Time: 15 minutes
Cooking Time: 30 minutes
Servings: 2

Ingredients:

- 1/4 cup butter
- 1/2 teaspoon mustard
- 1 tablespoon Worcestershire sauce
- Salt and pepper to taste
- 1/2 lb. steak strips

Method:

1. Set your toaster oven to broil.
2. In a bowl, mix the butter, mustard and Worcestershire sauce.
3. Sprinkle both sides of steak with salt and pepper.
4. Coat with the butter mixture.
5. Broil in the toaster oven for 15 minutes.
6. Brush both sides and flip.
7. Broil for another 15 minutes.

Serving Suggestion: Serve with mashed potatoes and gravy.

Preparation / Cooking Tips: You can also marinate the steak strips in the butter mixture for 30 minutes before cooking.

Herbed Beef Tenderloin

Preparation Time: 30 minutes

Cooking Time: 40 minutes

Servings: 6

Ingredients:

- 1 1/2 lb. beef tenderloin, sliced into strips
- Salt and pepper to taste
- 2 tablespoons mustard
- 3 cloves garlic
- 1 tablespoon fresh oregano, chopped
- 2 tablespoons fresh rosemary, chopped
- 2 tablespoons fresh thyme, chopped
- 1 teaspoon dried tarragon
- 3 tablespoons olive oil

Method:

1. Preheat your toaster oven to 375 degrees F.
2. Season beef with salt and pepper.
3. Rub it with mustard.
4. Add the remaining ingredients to a food processor.
5. Pulse until smooth.
6. Cover the steak strips with the herb mixture.
7. Bake in the toaster oven for 40 minutes.

Serving Suggestion: Let rest for 10 minutes before serving.

Preparation / Cooking Tips: Marinate the beef for 15 minutes before cooking.

Cheesesteak Sandwich

Preparation Time: 30 minutes

Cooking Time: 4 hours and 15 minutes

Servings: 4

Ingredients:

- 2 lb. beef strips
- 2 green bell peppers, sliced into strips
- 2 onions, sliced
- Salt to taste
- 4 tablespoons Italian salad dressing
- 1 cup beef stock
- 4 hoagie rolls, sliced into 2
- 4 slices cheddar cheese

Method:

1. Add the beef strips, onion and green bell peppers to a slow cooker.
2. Pour in beef stock.
3. Season with salt and Italian salad dressing.
4. Cook on low for 4 hours.
5. Set toaster oven to high.
6. Add the rolls to a baking pan.
7. Top the rolls with the beef mixture.
8. Place cheese slices on top.
9. Toast for 5 minutes.

Serving Suggestion: Serve with hot sauce or ketchup.

Preparation / Cooking Tips: Precook beef a few days before to make this dish in advance.

Glazed Pork Tenderloin

Preparation Time: 15 minutes

Cooking Time: 40 minutes

Servings: 4

Ingredients:

- Cooking spray
- 1 lb. pork tenderloin strips
- 1 teaspoon steak seasoning blend
- 1 onion, sliced into wedges
- 2 parsnips, sliced
- 2 carrots, sliced
- 1 tablespoon olive oil
- Salt and pepper to taste
- 1 tablespoon balsamic vinegar
- 1/2 cup apricot jam

Method:

1. Preheat your toaster oven to 425 degrees F.
2. Spray your baking pan with oil.
3. Season pork strips with seasoning blend.
4. Place pork strips in the middle of the pan.
5. In a bowl, toss onion, parsnips and carrots in olive oil.
6. Season with salt and pepper.
7. Add the vegetables around the pork tenderloin.
8. Bake in the toaster for 30 minutes.
9. Mix vinegar and apricot jam.
10. Drizzle mixture over the pork and veggies.
11. Bake for another 10 minutes.
12. Let cool and serve.

Serving Suggestion: Serve with the remaining sauce.

Preparation / Cooking Tips: Beef strips can also be used for this recipe.

Grilled Pork Belly

Preparation Time: 3 hours and 10 minutes

Cooking Time: 50 minutes

Servings: 6

Ingredients:

- 1 tablespoon lemon juice
- 1/2 cup soy sauce
- 1/2 cup ketchup
- 1 tablespoon garlic, minced
- Pepper to taste
- 3 lb. pork belly

Method:

1. Mix lemon juice, soy sauce, ketchup, garlic and pepper in a bowl.
2. Marinate the pork belly in the mixture for at least 3 hours, covered in the refrigerator.
3. Preheat toaster oven to 375 degrees F.
4. Put a grill rack inside the toaster oven.
5. Add the pork belly to the grill rack.
6. Cook for 20 minutes.
7. Flip and cook another 20 minutes.
8. Increase temperature to 450 degrees F.
9. Cook for 10 minutes.

Serving Suggestion: Serve with cucumber salad.

Preparation / Cooking Tips: Marinate overnight for tastier results.

Char Siu Pork

Preparation Time: 1 hour and 10 minutes
Cooking Time: 1 hour and 10 minutes
Servings: 4

Ingredients:

- 2 tablespoons soy sauce
- 1 tablespoon sugar
- 1 tablespoon red wine
- 1 tablespoon honey
- ¼ teaspoon Chinese five spice powder
- 1 teaspoon oyster sauce
- 1 teaspoon ginger, grated
- 1 lb. pork shoulder, sliced into cubes

Method:

1. Combine all ingredients in a bowl except pork.
2. Mix well.
3. Reserve 3 tablespoons of this mixture for basting.
4. Marinate pork in the remaining mixture for 1 hour.
5. Cook the pork in the toaster oven at 450 degrees F for 40 minutes.
6. Brush with the sauce.
7. Flip and cook for another 30 minutes.

Serving Suggestion: Serve with vegetable side dish.

Preparation / Cooking Tips: Bring pork to room temperature before cooking.

Cajun Pork Chops

Preparation Time: 40 minutes

Cooking Time: 40 minutes

Servings: 4

Ingredients:

- Cooking spray
- 4 pork chops
- Salt and pepper to taste
- 1 1/2 teaspoons paprika
- 1 1/2 teaspoons garlic powder
- 1 teaspoon dried thyme
- 1 teaspoon cayenne pepper

Method:

1. Preheat toaster oven to 375 degrees F.
2. Spray baking pan with oil.
3. Season pork chops with a mixture of salt, pepper, herbs and spices.
4. Bake pork chops for 40 minutes in the toaster oven, flipping once.

Serving Suggestion: Serve with hot sauce or ketchup.

Preparation / Cooking Tips: Marinate the pork chops for at least 30 minutes before cooking.

Garlic Herb Pork

Preparation Time: 15 minutes

Cooking Time: 35 minutes

Servings: 4

Ingredients:

- 3 cloves garlic
- 1 tablespoon fresh rosemary, chopped
- 1 tablespoon fresh parsley, chopped
- 1/2 tablespoon fresh thyme, chopped
- 2 tablespoons olive oil
- Salt to taste
- 4 pork chops

Method:

1. Preheat toaster oven to 450 degrees F.
2. Add garlic, herbs, oil and salt in a food processor.
3. Pulse until smooth.
4. Coat pork chops with this mixture.
5. Broil in the toaster oven for 15 to 20 minutes.
6. Flip and broil for another 15 minutes.

Serving Suggestion: Serve with steamed cauliflower or broccoli.

Preparation / Cooking Tips: Use boneless pork chop for this recipe.

Baked Pork Chops

Preparation Time: 15 minutes

Cooking Time: 30 minutes

Servings: 4

Ingredients:

- Cooking spray
- 2 tablespoons brown sugar
- 1/4 teaspoon onion powder
- 1/2 teaspoon garlic powder
- 1/2 teaspoon chili powder
- Salt and pepper to taste
- 4 pork chops
- 3 tablespoons olive oil

Method:

1. Preheat your toaster oven to 400 degrees F.
2. Spray your baking pan with oil.
3. In a bowl, mix the sugar, onion powder, garlic powder, chili powder, salt and pepper.
4. Brush both sides of pork with olive oil.
5. Sprinkle with sugar mixture.
6. Bake in the toaster oven for 20 to 30 minutes.

Serving Suggestion: Serve with fresh green salad.

Preparation / Cooking Tips: Use thick cut pork chops for this recipe.

Meatloaf

Preparation Time: 30 minutes

Cooking Time: 1 hour

Servings: 4

Ingredients:

- 1 1/2 lb. ground beef
- 1 1/2 lb. ground pork
- 2 onions, chopped
- 5 cloves garlic, chopped
- 1/2 cup milk
- 4 tablespoons breadcrumbs
- 1 cup fresh parsley, chopped
- 2 eggs, beaten
- Salt and pepper to taste

Method:

1. Preheat toaster oven to 350 degrees F.
2. Combine all the ingredients in a bowl.
3. Press mixture into a loaf pan.
4. Bake for 1 hour.

Serving Suggestion: Serve with rice or bread.

Preparation / Cooking Tips: Use lean ground beef and lean ground pork for this recipe.

Chapter 5: Poultry

Baked Crispy Chicken

Preparation Time: 15 minutes

Cooking Time: 1 hour

Servings: 6

Ingredients:

- 2 lb. chicken
- Vegetable oil
- Salt and pepper to taste
- 2 tablespoons flour
- 1/4 cup water

Method:

1. Coat chicken with oil.
2. Season with salt and pepper.
3. Dredge with flour.
4. Cook in the toaster oven at 400 degrees F for 1 hour.

Serving Suggestion: Serve with ketchup or gravy.

Preparation / Cooking Tips: You can also sprinkle chicken with dried rosemary for extra flavor.

Parmesan Chicken

Preparation Time: 20 minutes
Cooking Time: 20 minutes
Servings: 2

Ingredients:

- 2 chicken breast fillets
- Salt and pepper to taste
- 1 egg, beaten
- 3 tablespoons Parmesan cheese
- 1/2 cup breadcrumbs
- Pinch of paprika
- Vegetable oil
- 3 cloves garlic, minced
- 2 tomatoes, chopped
- 1/4 cup tomato paste
- 5 tablespoons mozzarella, shredded

Method:

1. Season chicken breast fillets with salt and pepper.
2. Add egg to a bowl.
3. In another bowl, mix Parmesan cheese, breadcrumbs and paprika.
4. Dip chicken in egg and then in Parmesan cheese mixture.
5. In a pan over medium heat, pour the oil and cook chicken until golden.
6. Transfer to a plate.
7. Pour oil into another bowl.
8. Cook garlic and tomatoes in the same pan.
9. Add tomato paste.
10. Cook for 2 minutes.
11. Spread tomato paste mixture in a small baking pan.

12. Place chicken on top.

13. Sprinkle with mozzarella cheese.

14. Bake in the toaster oven for 10 minutes.

Serving Suggestion: Garnish with fresh basil leaves.

Preparation / Cooking Tips: You can also dust chicken with flour before dipping into egg.

Garlic Chicken

Preparation Time: 4 hours and 15 minutes

Cooking Time: 20 minutes

Servings: 2

Ingredients:

- 1 tablespoon honey
- 1 tablespoon soy sauce
- 1 teaspoon sesame oil
- 2 chicken breast fillets
- Vegetable oil
- 1 teaspoon garlic powder
- 1 teaspoon dried oregano
- Salt and pepper to taste

Method:

1. Mix honey, soy sauce and sesame oil in a bowl.
2. Marinate the chicken in this mixture for 1 hour.
3. Grease a baking pan with oil.
4. Sprinkle chicken with garlic powder, oregano, salt and pepper.
5. Cook chicken in the toaster oven for 10 minutes per side.

Serving Suggestion: Serve with your favorite dipping sauce.

Preparation / Cooking Tips: You can marinate chicken for up to 4 hours.

Shredded Chicken

Preparation Time: 15 minutes

Cooking Time: 15 minutes

Servings: 2

Ingredients:

- 1/4 cup chicken, cooked and shredded
- 2 tablespoons garlic mayo sauce
- 2 tortillas
- 1/4 cup cheddar cheese, shredded
- 2 teaspoons Parmesan cheese

Method:

1. Mix shredded chicken and garlic mayo sauce in a bowl.
2. Top tortillas with this mixture.
3. Sprinkle cheddar and Parmesan cheese on top.
4. Roll up the tortillas.
5. Toast in the toaster oven for 15 minutes.

Serving Suggestion: Serve with green salad.

Preparation / Cooking Tips: You can also include chopped cabbage in the chicken mixture.

Chicken & Veggies with Rosemary

Preparation Time: 20 minutes

Cooking Time: 1 hour and 10 minutes

Servings: 4

Ingredients:

- 3 sprigs rosemary
- 1 onion, sliced into wedges
- 2 cloves garlic, peeled
- 1 sweet potato, sliced into cubes
- 1 parsnip, sliced into cubes
- 1 turnip, sliced into cubes
- 2 tablespoons olive oil
- Salt and pepper to taste
- 1/2 teaspoon garlic powder
- 4 chicken thighs

Method:

1. Preheat toaster oven to 425 degrees F.
2. Spray small baking pan with oil.
3. Put the rosemary in the pan.
4. In a bowl, toss the onion, garlic, sweet potato, parsnip and turnip in oil, salt and pepper.
5. Place veggies in the baking pan.
6. Bake in the toaster oven for 30 minutes.
7. Season chicken with salt, pepper and garlic powder.
8. Add chicken on top of vegetables. Bake for 40 minutes.

Serving Suggestion: Garnish with fresh rosemary sprigs before serving.

Preparation / Cooking Tips: You can also use other root vegetables for this recipe.

Baked Chicken Strips

Preparation Time: 15 minutes
Cooking Time: 20 minutes
Servings: 6

Ingredients:

- 2 teaspoons melted butter
- 2/3 cup breadcrumbs
- 2/3 cup crackers, crushed
- 2 eggs
- Salt and pepper to taste
- 1 1/2 lb. chicken strips

Method:

1. Preheat toaster oven to 450 degrees F.
2. Spray small baking pan with oil.
3. In a bowl, mix butter, breadcrumbs and crushed crackers.
4. In another bowl, beat the eggs and season with salt and pepper.
5. Dip chicken strip in egg mixture and then in butter mixture.
6. Arrange in a single layer in the baking pan.
7. Bake for 10 minutes per side.

Serving Suggestion: Serve with gravy or barbecue sauce.

Preparation / Cooking Tips: Prepare the chicken tenders in advance and freeze. Bake on the day you prefer to serve.

Chicken Casserole

Preparation Time: 30 minutes

Cooking Time: 30 minutes

Servings: 4

Ingredients:

- 4 cups chicken, cooked and sliced into cubes
- 2 cups cheddar cheese soup
- 3 cups spinach, chopped
- 1 cup light mayonnaise
- 1 cup milk
- 4 cups cooked pasta
- 2 cups Monterey Jack cheese, shredded
- 1 cup bacon, cooked crispy and chopped

Method:

1. Preheat your oven to 375 degrees F.
2. In a bowl, mix chicken, cheddar soup, spinach, mayo and milk.
3. Add pasta to a baking pan.
4. Pour chicken mixture on top.
5. Bake in the toaster oven for 20 minutes.
6. Sprinkle cheese and bacon on top.
7. Bake for another 10 minutes.

Serving Suggestion: Let cool before slicing and serving.

Preparation / Cooking Tips: You can also use mozzarella cheese for this recipe.

Cordon Bleu

Preparation Time: 15 minutes
Cooking Time: 20 minutes
Servings: 2

Ingredients:

- 2 chicken breast fillets
- 2 slices cheese
- 2 ham slices
- 1/2 cup all-purpose flour
- Salt and pepper to taste
- Pinch of paprika
- 1 egg
- 2 tablespoons milk
- 1/2 cup breadcrumbs
- 1 tablespoon canola oil
- 1 tablespoon melted butter

Method:

1. Flatten chicken breast with a meat mallet.
2. Top each chicken breast fillet with cheese and ham.
3. Roll up the chicken.
4. Mix flour, salt, pepper and paprika in a bowl.
5. In another bowl, beat egg. Stir in milk.
6. Add breadcrumbs to a third bowl.
7. Dip the chicken in the first, second and third bowls.
8. Coat with oil.
9. Bake in the toaster oven for 20 minutes.
10. Let cool before slicing and serving.

Serving Suggestion: Serve with mashed potato and gravy or fries.

Preparation / Cooking Tips: Prepare chicken cordon bleu in advance and freeze. Bake on the day you prefer to serve it.

Turkey Meatloaf

Preparation Time: 15 minutes
Cooking Time: 1 hour
Servings: 10

Ingredients:

- 2 lb. lean ground turkey
- 1 onion, chopped
- 1/2 cup carrot, shredded
- 1 cup quick-cooking oats
- 1/2 cup milk
- 1 teaspoon garlic powder
- 1/4 teaspoon pepper
- 2 tablespoons ketchup
- 1 egg

Method:

1. Preheat your oven to 350 degrees F.
2. Combine all the ingredients in a bowl.
3. Press mixture into a loaf pan.
4. Bake in the oven for 1 hour.

Serving Suggestion: Let cool for 10 minutes before serving.

Preparation / Cooking Tips: You can also add minced bell pepper to the mixture.

Baked Chicken Taters

Preparation Time: 15 minutes

Cooking Time: 35 minutes

Servings: 2

Ingredients:

- 1/2 cup milk
- 1/4 cup butter, sliced into cubes
- 2 cans cream of chicken soup
- 1 cup cheddar cheese, shredded
- 3 cups chicken, cooked and sliced into cubes
- 16 oz. frozen carrots and peas
- 32 oz. tater tots

Method:

1. In a pan over medium heat, mix milk, butter and soup.
2. Cook for 1 minute.
3. Stir in the cheese, chicken and vegetables.
4. Pour mixture into a baking pan.
5. Sprinkle tater tots on top.
6. Cook in the toaster oven at 400 degrees F for 30 minutes.

Serving Suggestion: Sprinkle with fresh herbs.

Preparation / Cooking Tips: Shredded cooked chicken can also be used for this recipe.

Chapter 6: Seafood

Mustard Salmon with Green Beans

Preparation Time: 30 minutes

Cooking Time: 15 minutes

Servings: 2

Ingredients:

- 2 salmon fillets
- 2 tablespoons olive oil
- 2 cloves garlic
- 1 tablespoon Dijon mustard
- 1 tablespoon soy sauce
- 1 yellow bell pepper, sliced into strips
- 1 red bell pepper, sliced into strips
- 1 leek, chopped
- 6 oz. green beans, trimmed
- Pepper to taste

Method:

1. Preheat toaster oven to 400 degrees F.
2. Spray baking pan with oil.
3. Add salmon to the pan.
4. Combine olive oil, garlic, mustard and soy sauce in a food processor.
5. Pulse until smooth.
6. In a bowl, toss the bell peppers, leeks and green beans in 1 tablespoon of mustard mixture.
7. Add to the pan beside the salmon.
8. Pour remaining mustard mixture on top of salmon.
9. Season with pepper.

10. Bake for 15 minutes.

Serving Suggestion: Serve with rice or pasta.

Preparation / Cooking Tips: You can also use other fish for this recipe.

Parmesan Fish Fillet

Preparation Time: 15 minutes

Cooking Time: 15 minutes

Servings: 2

Ingredients:

- 2 oz. Parmesan cheese, grated
- 1/4 cup breadcrumbs
- Pepper to taste
- 1/2 teaspoon Italian seasoning
- 1 tablespoon mayonnaise
- 2 fish fillets

Method:

1. Preheat your toaster oven to 425 degrees F.
2. Spray baking pan with oil.
3. In a bowl, mix the cheese, breadcrumbs, pepper and Italian seasoning.
4. Spread fish fillet with mayo.
5. Dredge with breadcrumb mixture.
6. Put the fish fillet in the baking pan.
7. Bake for 15 minutes.

Serving Suggestion: Serve with steamed veggies.

Preparation / Cooking Tips: Any white fish fillet can be used for this recipe.

Broiled Tilapia with Avocado

Preparation Time: 15 minutes
Cooking Time: 15 minutes
Servings: 2

Ingredients:

- 3 tablespoons sour cream
- 1 avocado, sliced in half and pitted
- 1 teaspoon lime juice
- 2 tilapia fillets
- 1 tablespoon mayonnaise
- Garlic salt

Method:

1. Add sour cream, avocado and lime juice to a food processor.
2. Pulse until smooth.
3. Transfer to a bowl.
4. Cover the bowl and refrigerate.
5. Spread fish fillet with mayo.
6. Sprinkle both sides with garlic salt.
7. Place in a baking pan.
8. Set your toaster oven to broil.
9. Broil for 10 to 15 minutes.
10. Serve with avocado and lime sauce.

Serving Suggestion: Garnish with chopped cilantro.

Preparation / Cooking Tips: Make sauce in advance to save time.

Walnut-Crusted Salmon

Preparation Time: 15 minutes

Cooking Time: 15 minutes

Servings: 2

Ingredients:

- 2 salmon fillets
- Salt and pepper to taste
- 3 tablespoons walnuts, chopped
- 2 tablespoons olive oil

Method:

1. Preheat your toaster oven to 400 degrees F.
2. Add salmon to a baking pan.
3. Season with salt and pepper.
4. Press walnuts onto the fish.
5. Brush with oil.
6. Bake in the toaster oven for 15 minutes.

Serving Suggestion: Serve with buttered corn and carrots.

Preparation / Cooking Tips: Toast walnuts in a pan over medium heat before using.

Pesto Salmon

Preparation Time: 15 minutes

Cooking Time: 15 minutes

Servings: 4

Ingredients:

- Cooking spray
- 4 salmon fillets
- 2 tablespoons white wine
- 2 tablespoons pesto
- 2 tablespoons pine nuts

Method:

1. Spray your baking pan with oil.
2. Add salmon fillet to the pan.
3. Drizzle with white wine.
4. Spread pesto and sprinkle with pine nuts.
5. Cook in the toaster oven at 400 degrees F for 15 minutes.

Serving Suggestion: Garnish with lemon wedges.

Preparation / Cooking Tips: Toast pine nuts before using.

Baked Cheesy Salmon

Preparation Time: 20 minutes

Cooking Time: 25 minutes

Servings: 2

Ingredients:

- 2 salmon fillets
- 1 tablespoon lemon juice
- Salt and pepper to taste
- 4 cloves garlic, minced
- 1/4 cup mayonnaise
- 1 teaspoon sugar
- 1 teaspoon liquid seasoning
- 1/4 cup mozzarella cheese, grated

Method:

1. Preheat toaster oven to 400 degrees F.
2. Brush both sides of salmon with lemon juice.
3. Sprinkle with salt, pepper and garlic.
4. Place in a baking pan.
5. In a bowl, mix the remaining ingredients except cheese.
6. Spread mixture on top of salmon.
7. Bake for 15 minutes.
8. Top with cheese.
9. Bake for 10 minutes.

Serving Suggestion: Garnish with fresh basil.

Preparation / Cooking Tips: You can also use cheddar cheese for this recipe.

Miso-Glazed Salmon

Preparation Time: 45 minutes

Cooking Time: 20 minutes

Servings: 4

Ingredients:

- 4 salmon fillets
- 1 tablespoon soy sauce
- 1/4 cup red wine
- 1/4 cup miso
- 1/4 cup sugar
- 2 tablespoons vegetable oil

Method:

1. Dry salmon with paper towels.
2. In a bowl, combine the rest of the ingredients.
3. Add salmon to the bowl.
4. Cover and marinate for 30 minutes.
5. Transfer to a small baking pan.
6. Preheat your toaster oven to 400 degrees F.
7. Set it to broil.
8. Cook for 15 to 20 minutes.

Serving Suggestion: Serve with fresh green salad.

Preparation / Cooking Tips: You can also reserve a few tablespoons of the mixture to be used as basting while broiling.

Lemon Butter Shrimp

Preparation Time: 15 minutes

Cooking Time: 25 minutes

Servings: 4

Ingredients:

- Cooking spray
- 1 1/2 lb. shrimp, peeled and deveined
- 1 teaspoon garlic powder
- 1/4 cup butter, melted
- 1/4 cup lemon juice

Method:

1. Preheat toaster oven to 450 degrees F.
2. Spray a small baking pan with oil.
3. Season shrimp with garlic powder.
4. Add to a baking pan.
5. Bake in the toaster oven for 15 minutes.
6. Mix butter and lemon juice in a bowl.
7. Pour mixture over the shrimp and bake for 10 minutes.

Serving Suggestion: Garnish with lemon wedges and chopped parsley.

Preparation / Cooking Tips: Fish can also be used for this recipe.

Broiled Salmon with Zucchini

Preparation Time: 15 minutes

Cooking Time: 15 minutes

Servings: 2

Ingredients:

- 2 salmon fillets
- 2 tablespoons olive oil, divided
- Salt and pepper to taste
- 1 zucchini, sliced

Method:

1. Set the toaster oven to broil.
2. Brush salmon with half of olive oil.
3. Season with salt and pepper.
4. Coat zucchini with remaining oil and sprinkle with salt and pepper.
5. Place zucchini and salmon in a baking pan.
6. Cook in the toaster oven for 10 to 15 minutes.

Serving Suggestion: Garnish with lime wedges.

Preparation / Cooking Tips: You can also drizzle salmon with lime juice before broiling.

Baked Sole & Asparagus

Preparation Time: 15 minutes
Cooking Time: 20 minutes
Servings: 2

Ingredients:

- Cooking spray
- 2 cups asparagus, trimmed and sliced
- 1 teaspoon olive oil
- Salt and pepper to taste
- 2 sole fillets
- Parmesan cheese, grated

Method:

1. Preheat toaster oven to 450 degrees F.
2. Spray baking pan with oil.
3. Put asparagus on one side.
4. Drizzle with oil and season with salt and pepper.
5. Add the sole fillets on the other side of the pan.
6. Brush with oil and sprinkle with salt and pepper.
7. Sprinkle with Parmesan cheese.
8. Bake for 15 to 20 minutes.

Serving Suggestion: Serve with mayo dipping sauce.

Preparation / Cooking Tips: Do not overcrowd the baking pan.

Chapter 7: Vegetable

Brussels Sprouts with Creamy Cheese Sauce

Preparation Time: 30 minutes
Cooking Time: 30 minutes
Servings: 6

Ingredients:

- 2 lb. Brussels sprouts
- 1 tablespoon olive oil
- Salt and pepper to taste
- 2 cloves garlic, chopped
- 3/4 cup sourdough bread, sliced into cubes
- 1 tablespoon fresh parsley, minced
- 1 tablespoon butter
- 1 cup all-purpose cream
- 1/8 teaspoon red pepper flakes
- 1/8 teaspoon ground nutmeg
- 1/2 cup cheddar cheese, shredded

Method:

1. Preheat your toaster oven to 450 degrees F.
2. Coat Brussels sprouts in oil, salt and pepper.
3. Place these in a baking pan.
4. Roast in the toaster oven for 10 minutes.
5. Add the garlic, bread, parsley and butter in a food processor.
6. Pulse until crumbly.
7. Stir in the remaining ingredients except cheese.
8. Spread mixture on top of Brussels sprouts.
9. Sprinkle cheese on top.

10. Reduce temperature to 400 degrees F.

11. Bake in the toaster oven for 20 minutes.

Serving Suggestion: Sprinkle dried herbs on top.

Preparation / Cooking Tips: Bake until surface is golden.

Veggie Stuffed Red Bell Peppers

Preparation Time: 30 minutes

Cooking Time: 1 hour

Servings: 6

Ingredients:

- 1 tablespoon olive oil
- 1 onion, chopped
- 1/4 green pepper, chopped
- 1 squash, chopped
- 1 zucchini, chopped
- 4 garlic cloves, crushed and minced
- 8 oz. tomato sauce
- 1 cup cooked white rice
- Salt to taste
- 1/2 cup mozzarella cheese
- 6 red bell peppers, tops sliced off and steamed
- 3 Provolone cheese slices

Method:

1. Preheat your toaster oven to 350 degrees F.
2. In a pan over medium heat, cook onion, green pepper and veggies in olive oil for 7 minutes.
3. Stir in garlic and spinach.
4. Cook for 1 minute.
5. Add tomato sauce, rice, salt and mozzarella cheese to the pan.
6. Stir and cook for 2 minutes.
7. Arrange red bell peppers in a small baking pan.
8. Stuff with the veggie mixture.
9. Bake for 40 minutes.

10. Put the provolone cheese on top.

11. Bake for 5 minutes.

Serving Suggestion: Serve as appetizer.

Preparation / Cooking Tips: You can also use brown rice for this recipe.

Roasted Snap Peas

Preparation Time: 10 minutes

Cooking Time: 10 minutes

Servings: 2

Ingredients:

- 8 oz. sugar snap peas
- 2 teaspoons olive oil
- 1 tablespoon shallot, chopped
- Salt to taste
- 1/2 teaspoon Italian seasoning

Method:

1. Preheat your toaster oven to 400 degrees F.
2. Combine all ingredients in a bowl.
3. Transfer to a small baking pan.
4. Roast in the oven for 10 minutes.

Serving Suggestion: Garnish with lemon wedges or chopped parsley.

Preparation / Cooking Tips: You can also replace snap peas with green beans.

Scalloped Potatoes

Preparation Time: 20 minutes

Cooking Time: 1 hour and 15 minutes

Servings: 6

Ingredients:

- 2 tablespoons butter
- 3 tablespoons all-purpose flour
- Salt and pepper to taste
- 1 1/2 cups milk
- 1/2 cup cheddar cheese, shredded
- 4 cups potatoes, sliced thinly
- 1 cup onion, sliced thinly

Method:

1. Preheat your toaster oven to 350 degrees F.
2. In a pan over medium heat, add butter and wait for it to melt.
3. Add flour and stir.
4. Sprinkle with salt and pepper.
5. Pour in milk.
6. Bring to a boil and then simmer for 2 minutes.
7. Stir in cheese.
8. Spray a small baking pan with oil.
9. Arrange the potatoes in the pan.
10. Layer with onion and cheese mixture.
11. Repeat layers.
12. Bake in the toaster oven for 1 hour.

Serving Suggestion: Sprinkle chopped fresh parsley on top.

Preparation / Cooking Tips: You can also pre-boil the potatoes and reduce cooking time in the toaster oven.

Buttered Cauliflower

Preparation Time: 15 minutes
Cooking Time: 55 minutes
Servings: 4

Ingredients:

- 6 cloves garlic
- 3 tablespoons butter
- 4 cups cauliflower florets
- Salt and pepper to taste
- 1/4 cup golden raisins
- 1/4 cup fresh parsley, chopped
- 1 tablespoon capers, chopped
- 2 teaspoons lemon juice

Method:

1. Preheat your toaster oven to 400 degrees F.
2. Wrap garlic cloves with foil.
3. Bake in the toaster oven for 30 minutes.
4. Peel garlic and mash. Set aside.
5. In a pan over medium heat, add butter and melt.
6. Arrange cauliflower in a small baking pan.
7. Drizzle with melted butter and season with salt and pepper.
8. Roast in the toaster oven for 20 minutes.
9. Transfer to a bowl.
10. Stir in garlic and the rest of ingredients.

Serving Suggestion: Garnish with herb sprigs.

Preparation / Cooking Tips: You can also roast garlic cloves without peeling.

Squash Mac & Cheese

Preparation Time: 15 minutes
Cooking Time: 30 minutes
Servings: 6

Ingredients:

- 8 oz. elbow macaroni
- 1 butternut squash, sliced into cubes and boiled
- 1 cup milk
- 1/4 cup Greek yogurt
- Pinch ground nutmeg
- Salt and pepper to taste
- 6 oz. cheddar cheese, shredded
- 1/2 cup Parmesan cheese, shredded
- 1/2 cup breadcrumbs

Method:

1. Cook elbow macaroni according to the directions in the package.
2. Drain and set aside.
3. Preheat your toaster oven to 400 degrees F.
4. Add squash, milk, yogurt, nutmeg, salt and pepper in a food processor.
5. Pulse until pureed.
6. Add to a pan over medium heat.
7. Stir in cheddar and Parmesan cheese.
8. Cook for 3 minutes.
9. Add pasta to a small baking pan.
10. Pour squash mixture on top.
11. Toss to coat evenly.
12. Sprinkle breadcrumbs on top.
13. Bake in the toaster oven for 20 minutes.

Serving Suggestion: Sprinkle with pepper and dried herbs before serving.

Preparation / Cooking Tips: Use whole-wheat elbow macaroni.

Asparagus Strata

Preparation Time: 1 hour and 15 minutes

Cooking Time: 1 hour

Servings: 6

Ingredients:

- 5 eggs
- 1/2 cup cream
- 2 cups almond milk
- Pinch of ground nutmeg
- Salt and pepper to taste
- 4 cups Italian bread, sliced into cubes
- 1 cup asparagus, trimmed and sliced
- 1 1/4 cups Monterey Jack cheese

Method:

1. Beat eggs in a bowl.
2. Stir in the rest of the ingredients.
3. Pour mixture into a small baking pan.
4. Cover and refrigerate for 1 hour.
5. Preheat your toaster oven to 325 degrees F.
6. Bake for 20 minutes.
7. Cover with foil and bake for another 40 minutes.

Serving Suggestion: Sprinkle pepper on top before serving.

Preparation / Cooking Tips: You can also top with additional cheese before baking for 40 minutes.

Paprika Cauliflower Bites

Preparation Time: 10 minutes

Cooking Time: 20 minutes

Servings: 4

Ingredients:

- 3 tablespoons olive oil
- 1 teaspoon paprika
- 1/8 teaspoon chili powder
- 1/4 teaspoon ground turmeric
- 1/2 teaspoon ground cumin
- Salt to taste
- 4 cups cauliflower florets

Method:

1. Preheat your toaster oven to 450 degrees F.
2. Combine oil with spices and salt.
3. Stir in cauliflower florets.
4. Coat evenly with mixture.
5. Pour into a small baking pan.
6. Roast for 20 minutes.

Serving Suggestion: Serve as appetizer.

Preparation / Cooking Tips: Use Spanish-style paprika.

Vegetable Casserole

Preparation Time: 15 minutes

Cooking Time: 25 minutes

Servings: 4

Ingredients:

- 2 teaspoons butter
- 1/4 cup breadcrumbs
- 2 tablespoons butter
- 1 1/2 cups milk
- 2 tablespoons all-purpose flour
- 1/2 cup Parmesan cheese, grated
- 3/4 cup cheddar cheese, shredded
- 16 oz. broccoli florets, steamed
- 16 oz. cauliflower florets, steamed

Method:

1. Preheat your toaster oven to 425 degrees F.
2. In a pan over medium heat, add 2 teaspoons butter and breadcrumbs. Cook for 3 minutes.
3. Transfer to a bowl. Set aside.
4. Add remaining butter to the pan.
5. Add milk, flour and cheeses.
6. Bring to a boil. Simmer for 3 minutes.
7. Turn off the stove.
8. Stir in veggies.
9. Pour mixture into a small baking pan.
10. Sprinkle buttered breadcrumbs on top.
11. Bake in the toaster oven for 15 minutes.

Serving Suggestion: Sprinkle with salt and pepper to taste

Preparation / Cooking Tips: You can also use almond milk for this recipe.

Mushroom Casserole

Preparation Time: 15 minutes
Cooking Time: 35 minutes
Servings: 6

Ingredients:

- 14 oz. chicken broth
- 3 tablespoons cornstarch
- Salt and pepper to taste
- 1 tablespoon butter
- 1/4 cup onion, chopped
- 1 garlic clove, crushed and minced
- 12 oz. evaporated milk
- 3 cups cooked spaghetti
- 3 cups mushrooms
- 2 tablespoons Parmesan cheese, grated

Method:

1. Preheat your toaster oven to 350 degrees F.
2. In a bowl, mix chicken broth, cornstarch, salt and pepper.
3. Add butter to a pan over medium heat.
4. Cook onion and garlic for 3 minutes.
5. Stir in broth mixture
6. Bring to a boil and then simmer for 2 minutes.
7. Pour in milk, spaghetti and mushrooms.
8. Pour mixture to a small baking pan.
9. Bake for 20 minutes.
10. Sprinkle cheese on top.
11. Bake for 5 minutes.

Serving Suggestion: Sprinkle chopped parsley on top before serving.

Preparation / Cooking Tips: Use low-sodium chicken broth. If you prefer a vegetarian dish, use vegetable stock instead.

Chapter 8: Snack / Appetizer

Asparagus Fries

Preparation Time: 15 minutes

Cooking Time: 15 minutes

Servings: 4

Ingredients:

- 1 1/2 cups mayonnaise
- 2 cloves garlic, crushed and minced
- 3/4 cup Parmesan cheese, grated
- 1 tablespoon Italian seasoning
- 1 tablespoon dried parsley
- Salt and pepper to taste
- 1/2 lb. thick asparagus, trimmed
- 1 cup breadcrumbs

Method:

1. Preheat your toaster oven to 425 degrees F.
2. In a bowl, mix the mayo, garlic, Parmesan cheese, Italian seasoning, parsley, salt and pepper.
3. Take 1 cup of the mixture and reserve for later.
4. Coat the asparagus with the remaining mayo mixture and then dredge with breadcrumbs.
5. Arrange on a small baking pan.
6. Bake for 15 minutes.
7. Serve with reserved mayo dip.

Serving Suggestion: You can also serve with ketchup.

Preparation / Cooking Tips: Bake for 15 minutes or until asparagus are crispy.

Parmesan-Crusted Peas

Preparation Time: 15 minutes

Cooking Time: 15 minutes

Servings: 4

Ingredients:

- 1 clove garlic, crushed and minced
- 3 tablespoons olive oil
- 2 cups peas
- 1/2 cup Parmesan cheese, shredded

Method:

1. Preheat your toaster oven to 350 degrees F.
2. Toss garlic in oil.
3. Place in a small baking pan.
4. Bake in the toaster oven for 5 minutes.
5. Stir in peas.
6. Bake for 10 minutes.
7. Sprinkle with Parmesan cheese.

Serving Suggestion: Sprinkle with pepper on top before serving.

Preparation / Cooking Tips: You can also roast whole garlic cloves and then mash to form a paste and mix with peas.

Cajun Okra

Preparation Time: 15 minutes
Cooking Time: 40 minutes
Servings: 4

Ingredients:

- Cooking spray
- 1 lb. okra, sliced lengthwise
- 1 teaspoon Cajun seasoning
- 2 tablespoons olive oil
- Salt and pepper to taste

Method:

1. Preheat your toaster oven to 450 degrees F.
2. Spray a small baking pan with oil.
3. Combine all the ingredients in the baking pan.
4. Coat evenly with the mixture.
5. Bake in the toaster oven for 40 minutes.

Serving Suggestion: Serve with Cajun dipping sauce.

Preparation / Cooking Tips: You can also marinate the okra for 30 minutes before baking.

Chicken Nachos

Preparation Time: 15 minutes
Cooking Time: 30 minutes
Servings: 4

Ingredients:

- Cooking spray
- Tortilla chips
- 2 cups chicken, cooked and shredded
- 2 cups salsa, divided
- 2 cups Monterey Jack cheese, shredded and divided
- 1 fresh jalapeno, sliced
- 1 cup black beans, rinsed and drained

Method:

1. Preheat toaster oven to 350 degrees F.
2. Spray small baking pan with oil.
3. Arrange the chips in the baking pan.
4. Top with the remaining ingredients, reserving 1 cup salsa for dip and 1 cup cheese for topping.
5. Bake in the toaster oven for 20 minutes.
6. Sprinkle cheese on top and bake for another 10 minutes.
7. Serve with reserved salsa.

Serving Suggestion: Serve with sour cream and guacamole.

Preparation / Cooking Tips: You can also use cooked lean ground beef for this recipe.

Roasted Pumpkin Seeds

Preparation Time: 5 minutes

Cooking Time: 50 minutes

Servings: 4

Ingredients:

- 4 cups pumpkin seeds
- 1 tablespoon olive oil
- Salt to taste

Method:

1. Preheat your toaster oven to 300 degrees F.
2. Spread pumpkin seeds on a small baking pan.
3. Roast in the toaster oven for 30 minutes.
4. Coat seeds with olive oil and season with salt.
5. Roast for another 20 minutes.

Serving Suggestion: Store in airtight container for up to 1 week.

Preparation / Cooking Tips: You can also sprinkle seeds with cinnamon powder or ranch dressing before roasting.

Baked Sweet Potatoes

Preparation Time: 20 minutes

Cooking Time: 1 hour and 30 minutes

Servings: 6

Ingredients:

- 6 sweet potatoes
- 2 tablespoons butter
- Garlic powder to taste
- 1 tablespoon fresh parsley, chopped

Method:

1. Preheat your toaster oven to 450 degrees F.
2. Poke the sweet potatoes with fork.
3. Place sweet potatoes in a small baking pan.
4. Bake for 1 hour.
5. Brush with butter and sprinkle with garlic powder and parsley.
6. Bake for another 30 minutes.

Serving Suggestion: Let cool and slice before serving.

Preparation / Cooking Tips: You can also use dried parsley for this recipe.

Bruschetta

Preparation Time: 15 minutes

Cooking Time: 5 minutes

Servings: 6

Ingredients:

- 4 cups fresh basil leaves
- 3 cloves garlic
- 1/2 cup pine nuts
- 1/2 cup Parmesan cheese
- 2 tablespoons balsamic vinegar
- 1 Italian bread loaf, sliced
- 2 tomatoes, chopped
- Salt and pepper to taste

Method:

1. Add basil, garlic, pine nuts, Parmesan cheese and vinegar to a food processor.
2. Pulse until smooth.
3. Spread basil mixture on top of the bread slices.
4. Top with the chopped tomatoes.
5. Sprinkle with salt and pepper.
6. Toast in the toaster oven for 5 minutes.

Serving Suggestion: Garnish with basil leaf on top of each bread.

Preparation / Cooking Tips: You can also use walnuts instead of pine nuts.

Yogurt Cornbread

Preparation Time: 20 minutes

Cooking Time: 30 minutes

Servings: 8

Ingredients:

- 1/4 cup all-purpose flour
- 1 cup yellow cornmeal
- 2 teaspoons baking powder
- 1/4 teaspoon baking soda
- Pinch salt
- 1 egg, beaten
- 1/2 cup milk
- 1 cup yogurt
- 1 tablespoon honey
- 1/4 cup oil

Method:

1. In a bowl, mix the flour, cornmeal, baking powder, baking soda and salt.
2. In another bowl, combine the remaining ingredients.
3. Add the second bowl to the first one. Mix well.
4. Pour into a small baking pan.
5. Bake in the toaster oven at 350 degrees F for 20 to 30 minutes.

Serving Suggestion: Let cool before slicing and serving.

Preparation / Cooking Tips: Use low-fat plain yogurt.

Pepperoni Bites

Preparation Time: 15 minutes

Cooking Time: 10 minutes

Servings: 8

Ingredients:

- 8 oz. crescent rolls, sliced
- 16 pepperoni slices
- 2 oz. string cheese, sliced
- Garlic salt to taste

Method:

1. Unroll the dough.
2. Add pepperoni slices and cheese on top.
3. Season with garlic salt.
4. Roll them up.
5. Bake in the toaster oven at 375 degrees F for 10 minutes.

Serving Suggestion: Serve warm.

Preparation / Cooking Tips: Brush with oil and sprinkle with garlic salt before baking.

Lentil Loaf

Preparation Time: 30 minutes

Cooking Time: 1 hour and 40 minutes

Servings: 6

Ingredients:

- 14 oz. vegetable broth
- 3/4 cup brown lentils, rinsed and drained
- Cooking spray
- 1 tablespoon olive oil
- 1 cup onion, chopped
- 1 cup mushrooms, chopped
- 2 cups carrots, shredded
- 1 tablespoon fresh parsley, minced
- 2 tablespoons fresh basil, minced
- 1 cup mozzarella, shredded
- 1/2 cup cooked brown rice
- 1 egg
- 1 egg white
- Salt and pepper to taste
- 1/2 teaspoon garlic powder
- 2 tablespoons tomato paste
- 2 tablespoons water

Method:

1. Pour broth into a pot over medium heat.
2. Add lentil and bring to a boil.
3. Reduce heat and simmer for 30 minutes.
4. Drain and set aside.

5. Preheat your toaster oven to 350 degrees F.

6. Spray your loaf pan with oil.

7. In a pan over medium heat, cook onion, mushrooms and carrots for 10 minutes.

8. Season with herbs.

9. Transfer to a bowl.

10. Stir in the rest of the ingredients along with the cooked lentils.

11. Mix and pour mixture into the loaf pan.

12. Bake in the toaster oven for 50 minutes.

Serving Suggestion: Let sit for 10 minutes before slicing and serving.

Preparation / Cooking Tips: You can also use 2 eggs instead of 1 egg and 1 egg white.

Chapter 9: Dessert

Sweetened Grapefruit

Preparation Time: 5 minutes

Cooking Time: 5 minutes

Servings: 2

Ingredients:

- 2 teaspoons brown sugar
- 2 tablespoons granulated sugar
- 1 grapefruit, sliced in half
- Pinch salt

Method:

1. In a bowl, mix the 2 sugars.
2. Sprinkle on top of the grapefruit.
3. Set your toaster oven to broil.
4. Broil the grapefruit for 5 minutes.
5. Sprinkle with salt and serve.

Serving Suggestion: Garnish with fresh mint leaves.

Preparation / Cooking Tips: You can also use this recipe for other fruits.

Peanut Butter Cookies

Preparation Time: 20 minutes

Cooking Time: 20 minutes

Servings: 4

Ingredients:

- 1 1/2 cups all-purpose flour
- 1 teaspoon baking soda
- 1/2 cup peanut butter
- 1/2 cup vegetable shortening
- 1 egg, beaten
- 1 1/4 cups brown sugar
- 1 teaspoon vanilla
- Pinch salt

Method:

1. Preheat your toaster oven to 275 degrees F.
2. Combine all the ingredients in a bowl.
3. Mix well.
4. Form cookies from the mixture and place in a small cookie sheet.
5. Bake for 20 minutes.

Serving Suggestion: Let cool on a wire rack before serving.

Preparation / Cooking Tips: Use natural and organic peanut butter for best results.

Chocolate & Vanilla Cookies

Preparation Time: 20 minutes

Cooking Time: 15 minutes

Servings: 6

Ingredients:

- 2 cups all-purpose flour
- 2 cups rolled oats
- 1 cup butter
- 2 eggs
- 1 cup brown sugar
- 1 cup sugar
- ½ teaspoon baking powder
- 1 teaspoon baking soda
- ½ teaspoon salt
- 1 tablespoon vanilla
- 12 oz. chocolate chips

Method:

1. Preheat your toaster oven to 350 degrees F.
2. Combine all the ingredients in a bowl.
3. Form cookies from the mixture.
4. Arrange on a small cookie sheet.
5. Bake in the toaster oven for 15 minutes.

Serving Suggestion: Let cool on a wire rack before serving.

Preparation / Cooking Tips: Use a mixer to make the baking process more convenient.

Peach Cobbler

Preparation Time: 20 minutes

Cooking Time: 45 minutes

Servings: 8

Ingredients:

- 1/4 cup cornstarch
- 1/2 cup brown sugar
- 2 tablespoons lemon juice
- 8 peaches, sliced in half
- 1 1/4 cups all-purpose flour
- 1 teaspoon ginger, grated
- 1 teaspoon lemon zest
- 1/2 cup sugar
- 3 tablespoons milk
- 1/2 cup melted butter
- Salt to taste

Method:

1. Preheat your toaster oven to 350 degrees F.
2. Mix the cornstarch, brown sugar and lemon juice in a bowl.
3. Coat peaches with this mixture and place on a small baking dish.
4. In another bowl, mix the remaining ingredients.
5. Pour mixture on top of the peaches.
6. Bake for 45 minutes.

Serving Suggestion: Garnish with fresh mint leaves.

Preparation / Cooking Tips: Use freshly squeezed lemon juice.

Brownie Cookies

Preparation Time: 20 minutes

Cooking Time: 10 minutes

Servings: 6

Ingredients:

- 1 1/2 cups light brown sugar
- 2/3 cup shortening
- 2 eggs, beaten
- 1 teaspoon vanilla
- 1 tablespoon water
- 1 1/4 cups all-purpose flour
- 1/4 teaspoon baking soda
- 1/3 cup unsweetened baking cocoa
- 12 oz. chocolate chips
- Pinch salt

Method:

1. Preheat your toaster oven to 375 degrees F.
2. In a bowl, mix brown sugar and shortening.
3. Stir in eggs, vanilla and water.
4. Slowly add the remaining ingredients.
5. Form cookies from the mixture.
6. Bake for 10 minutes.

Serving Suggestion: Let cool on a wire rack before serving.

Preparation / Cooking Tips: Use dark chocolate chips for this recipe.

Choco Chip Cookies

Preparation Time: 20 minutes

Cooking Time: 15 minutes

Servings: 16

Ingredients:

- 1 1/2 cups all-purpose flour
- 1 teaspoon baking powder
- 1 egg
- 1 tablespoon milk
- 1/2 cup shortening
- 1/4 cup granulated sugar
- 1/2 cup brown sugar
- Pinch salt
- 1 cup chocolate chips

Method:

1. Preheat your toaster oven to 375 degrees F.
2. Combine all ingredients except chocolate chips in a bowl.
3. Use a mixer to beat ingredients on medium speed.
4. Fold in chocolate chips.
5. Form cookies from the mixture and arrange on a small cookie pan.
6. Bake for 10 to 15 minutes.

Serving Suggestion: Let cool on a wire rack before serving.

Preparation / Cooking Tips: Use dark brown sugar for this recipe.

Apple & Carrot Muffins

Preparation Time: 30 minutes

Cooking Time: 30 minutes

Servings: 10

Ingredients:

- 2 cups all-purpose flour
- 1 1/2 teaspoons baking powder
- 1/4 cup oil
- 1 cup milk
- 4 carrots, grated
- 1 apple, grated
- 1/2 cup applesauce
- 3 eggs, beaten
- 1/4 cup white sugar
- 2 teaspoons cinnamon powder
- 1 teaspoon vanilla extract
- Pinch salt

Method:

1. Combine all the ingredients in a bowl.
2. Pour mixture into a muffin pan.
3. Bake in the toaster oven at 400 degrees F for 25 to 30 minutes.

Serving Suggestion: Let cool and serve.

Preparation / Cooking Tips: Use natural applesauce for this recipe.

Mug Cake

Preparation Time: 20 minutes
Cooking Time: 20 minutes
Serving: 1

Ingredients:

- 1/4 cup all-purpose flour
- 1/4 teaspoon baking powder
- 1/8 teaspoon baking soda
- 2 tablespoons sugar
- Pinch of salt
- 2 tablespoons applesauce
- 2 tablespoons milk
- 1/2 tablespoon vegetable oil
- 1/4 teaspoon vanilla extract
- 2 tablespoons chocolate chips

Method:

1. Preheat your toaster oven to 375 degrees F.
2. Mix the flour, baking powder, baking soda, sugar and salt in a bowl.
3. In another bowl, combine the remaining ingredients.
4. Slowly add second bowl to the first one.
5. Mix well.
6. Pour into an oven-safe mug.
7. Bake for 15 to 20 minutes.

Serving Suggestion: Serve with vanilla ice cream.

Preparation / Cooking Tips: Insert toothpick and when it comes out clean, it's already done.

Donuts

Preparation Time: 20 minutes

Cooking Time: 15 minutes

Servings: 6

Ingredients:

- 1 cup all-purpose flour
- 1/3 cup granulated sugar
- 1 1/2 teaspoons baking powder
- 2 tablespoons melted butter
- 1/2 cup buttermilk
- 1 egg
- 1 tablespoon vanilla extract
- Pinch of salt

Method:

1. Preheat your toaster oven to 350 degrees F.
2. In a bowl, combine all the ingredients.
3. Pour mixture into a donut pan.
4. Bake for 15 to 20 minutes.

Serving Suggestion: You can also dip donuts in chocolate sauce before serving.

Preparation / Cooking Tips: Consume within 3 days.

Blueberry Loaf Cake

Preparation Time: 20 minutes

Cooking Time: 1 hour and 20 minutes

Servings: 5

Ingredients:

- Cooking spray
- Vegetable oil
- 2 cups all-purpose flour
- 3/4 cup white sugar
- 2 teaspoons lemon zest
- 1 1/2 teaspoons baking powder
- 1/4 teaspoon salt
- 2 eggs, beaten
- 1/2 cup melted butter
- 1/2 cup milk
- 1 cup blueberries
- 1/2 cup walnuts, chopped

Method:

1. Preheat your toaster oven to 350 degrees F.
2. Grease your loaf pan with oil.
3. Combine all the ingredients in a bowl.
4. Pour into the loaf pan.
5. Bake in the toaster oven for 1 hour and 20 minutes.

Serving Suggestion: Let cool on wire rack before serving.

Preparation / Cooking Tips: You can use frozen or fresh blueberries.

Conclusion

Modern toasters have evolved from solely cooking breakfast favorites to churning out full set meals and desserts.

It is the optimal choice for people living alone, students, couples, young families, and the elderly. One of the best things about the good old oven toaster is that it is portable and does not need to be installed or fixed into a designated portion in your kitchen.

It can be used comfortably by the young and old alike and eliminates the hassle of ducking or stooping down since toaster ovens sit conveniently on countertops.

Oven toasters are useful appliances that are multi-function and are much cheaper than full-sized kitchen ovens. They may be smaller, but they are efficient in cooking and consume less time, energy consumption, and carbon footprint.

There are various types of toaster ovens available in the market with varying prices to suit any budget. Whatever your preference and needs, you can choose from standard, infrared, convection, or combination oven toasters.

Oven toasters are excellent back-up cookers even if you already own a conventional oven. It proves to be useful whenever you need to cook smaller servings of dishes or need to re-heat leftovers quickly. They come in handy in providing extra cooking room if you have exhausted your conventional oven.

If you are someone who loves baking and cooking but does not have enough kitchen space to accommodate a full-sized oven, getting a toaster oven is the next best choice for you. They are practical alternatives to bulky appliances that use up more power and demand more upkeep.

CPSIA information can be obtained
at www.ICGtesting.com
Printed in the USA
LVHW100806021120
670426LV00010B/384

9 781953 702876